THE AMERICAN WEST
Images of Past and Present

Out where the handclasp's a little stronger,
Out where the smile dwells a little longer,
    That's where the West begins;
Out where the sun is a little brighter,
Where the snows that fall are a trifle whiter,
Where the bonds of home are a wee bit tighter,
    That's where the West begins.

Out where the skies are a trifle bluer,
Out where friendship's a little truer,
    That's where the West begins;
Out where a fresher breeze is blowing,
Where there's laughter in every streamlet flowing,
Where there's more of reaping and less of sowing,
    That's where the West begins.

Out where the world is in the making,
Where fewer hearts in despair are aching,
    That's where the West begins;
Where there's more of singing and less of sighing,
Where there's more of giving and less of buying,
And man makes friends without half trying,
    That's where the West begins.

Arthur Chapman

This book was devised and produced by
Multimedia Publications (UK) Ltd

Editor: Anthony J. Lambert
Production: Arnon Orbach
Design: John Strange and Associates
Picture Research: Veneta Bullen

First published in the United States of
America 1985 by Gallery Books, an imprint of
W. H. Smith Publishers Inc., 112 Madison
Avenue, New York, NY 10016

ISBN 0 8317 0299 0

Typeset by Flowery Typesetters Ltd
Origination by Reprollovet, Spain
Printed in Italy by New Interlitho SpA, Milan

THE AMERICAN
WEST
Images of Past and Present

Tim Newark

GALLERY BOOKS
An Imprint of W. H. Smith Publishers Inc.
112 Madison Avenue
New York City 10016

Contents

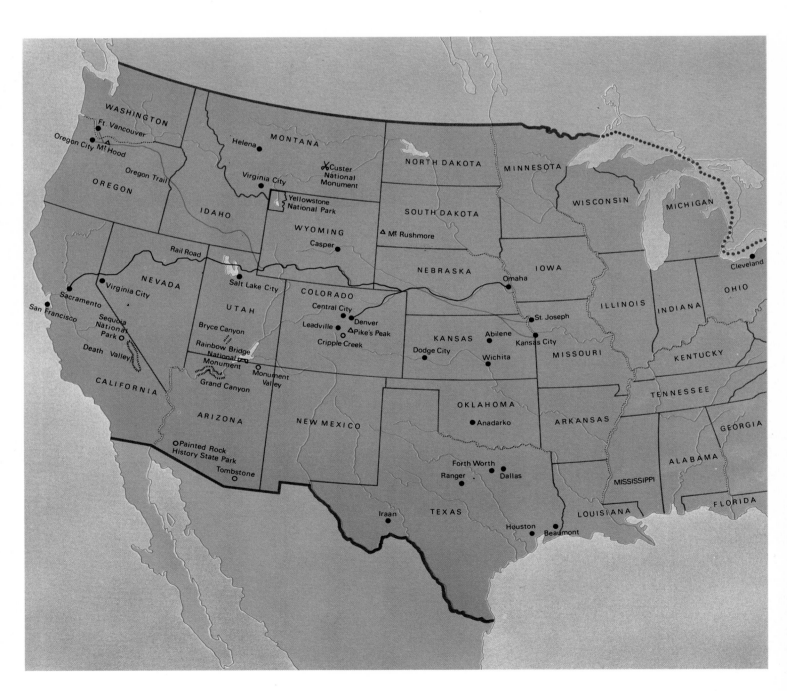

WASHINGTON

Ft. Vancouver
Oregon City Mt Hood
Oregon Trail

OREGON

Helena

MONTANA

Virginia City

Custer
National
Monument

Yellowstone
National Park

IDAHO

WYOMING

Casper

Rail Road

NEVADA

Virginia City

Salt Lake City

COLORADO

Central City

Sacramento

UTAH

Denver

San Francisco

Sequoia
National
Park

Bryce Canyon

Leadville
Cripple Creek

Pike's Peak

Death Valley

Rainbow Bridge
National
Monument

CALIFORNIA

Grand Canyon

Monument
Valley

ARIZONA

NEW MEXICO

Painted Rock
History State Park

Tombstone

NORTH DAKOTA

MINNESOTA

SOUTH DAKOTA

WISCONSIN

MICHIGAN

Mt Rushmore

Cleveland

NEBRASKA

IOWA

Omaha

OHIO

ILLINOIS

INDIANA

St. Joseph

KANSAS

Abilene

Kansas City

MISSOURI

KENTUCKY

Dodge City

Wichita

OKLAHOMA

ARKANSAS

TENNESSEE

Anadarko

GEORGIA

Forth Worth

Ranger

Dallas

ALABAMA

MISSISSIPPI

FLORIDA

Iraan

TEXAS

LOUISIANA

Houston
Beaumont

Introduction

When the United States gained independence in 1783, the western boundary of the new nation was established at the Mississippi River. Beyond that was a wilderness of wild animals, savage Indians and vast tracts of untamed land. In 1803 President Thomas Jefferson made the Louisiana Purchase. For an agreed sum of 15 million dollars, he doubled the size of the young republic with land stretching from the Mississippi to the Rocky Mountains. Soon after, hardy pioneers, daring fur trappers and optimistic gold miners blazed trails into the new territory. The winning of the West had begun.

In 1845 the Republic of Texas joined the United States, which led to war with Mexico. But the Americans triumphed and Mexico was forced to relinquish all claims to the land that now forms the states of Arizona, New Mexico, Utah, Nevada and California. Texas became a key element in the development of the West. Here the cowboy was born. Driving huge herds of longhorn cattle northwards, the era of Wild West towns and legendary characters had arrived. This is the image of the Old West that has endured over a hundred years and kept alive the excitement of the frontier in popular culture.

The opening of the Indian Territory of Oklahoma to white homesteaders in 1889 was the beginning of the end of the Old West. A frontier line no longer existed. From the Pacific to the Mississippi, from Montana to Texas, railroads and settlers had brought the wilderness under control. But the pioneer spirit lives on. The American West is a place where the imagination can roam unhindered across wide open plains and amongst magnificent natural grandeur. It remains a symbol of adventure and enterprise, and above all, freedom.

1. The Indian Heritage

At a dinner in 1909 in honor of Buffalo Bill Cody, it was proposed that a heroic Indian statue be erected at the mouth of New York Harbor. This memorial to "The First Americans", to be sculpted by the great Western artist Frederic Remington, would confront all ships entering the port "so that when the foreigner comes," explained another artist, "there his eyes will rest upon a fine group as big or bigger than the Statue of Liberty, of Remington Indians welcoming him to America." Unfortunately, Remington died that very year and the project was never carried out. High in the Black Hills of South Dakota, however, there is a massive monument worthy of America's Indian heritage.

Seeing the gigantic heads of four American Presidents carved out of the granite face of Mount Rushmore, Chief Henry Standing Bear asked Korczak Ziolkowski to carve a mountain memorial to Chief Crazy Horse "to remind the white people that the Indians also had great leaders". The grand idea fired Ziolkowski's imagination and he promised to carve the memorial out of the Black Hills, sacred to the Sioux. Using power drill and dynamite to blast away the rock, the monument will be the largest statue in the world. Ziolkowski began his mammoth endeavor in 1948, and his family now carry on the late sculptor's dream. Despite Hollywood's almost relentless portrayal of the American Indian as a villain, the United States is beginning to acknowledge the importance of its Indian legacy.

Although there are many different cultural groups among the Indians, it is the Plains Indian who best symbolizes the American Red Indian: the proud warrior in feather war bonnet mounted on his painted pony high on a bluff, ready to swoop like an eagle upon his enemy. And of all the Plains Indians, it is the Sioux who are most renowned for their stiff resistance to the white settlers. Their struggle to keep their land produced many notable Indian heroes. Red Cloud, chief of the Oglala Sioux, was one of the most successful. So named because the sky turned red at the time of his birth, Red Cloud was described by General George Crook, the outstanding Indian fighter, as a "magnificent specimen of physical manhood, as full of action as a tiger".

In the summer of 1865, the US Army began to build and garrison forts on the Bozeman Trail. This ran through the Sioux country to the goldfields of Montana. Red Cloud protested against this invasion but the government ignored him. So he went to war. He constantly harassed the trail and its forts, keeping the largest post under virtual siege. When Captain Fetterman and 80 soldiers rode out to rescue a woodcutting party under attack near the fort in 1866, Red Cloud's warriors lured Fetterman into an ambush,

killing him and every member of his command.

Red Cloud waged his war so effectively that, in 1868, the US government was forced to negotiate a treaty and yield to his demands that the forts be abandoned and the troops withdrawn completely. Red Cloud refused to sign the treaty until the soldiers had left the Powder River country and his warriors had burned the forts to the ground. On signing the Fort Laramie Treaty, creating the vast area known as the Great Sioux Reservation, the triumphant Oglala chief agreed to settle peacefully on the Red Cloud Agency in Nebraska. A man of his word, he took no part in the Sioux hostilities of the 1870s, although he remained a forceful critic of the government and its often corrupt Indian agents.

Previous page
Monument Valley on the borders of Arizona and Utah.

Opposite
Chief Sitting Bull of the Hunkpapa Sioux painted by Robert Lindneux. The most celebrated chief and medicine man of the great Sioux nation, he predicted the sensational defeat of General Custer.

Below
High in the Black Hills of South Dakota stands a monument to one man's dream and a proud Indian nation, the Crazy Horse Monument. Begun by Korczak Ziolkowski, it is now being completed by his family at Thunderhead Mountain, five miles north of Custer.

By the end of 1868 nearly half the Sioux nation was resigned to reservation life. But Chief Sitting Bull and his Hunkpapas remained free in the buffalo country. Like all Plains Indians, the Sioux were buffalo hunters who depended on the huge shaggy beasts for food, clothing, shelter, tools and equipment. They used every part of the buffalo, wasting nothing. In 1875 the US government directed all Sioux Indians to enter reservations by the end of January 1876 or be declared hostile. Many bands of Sioux did not meet this deadline and were attacked by US troops. Chief Crazy Horse and his Oglala followers joined forces with Sitting Bull. By the spring of 1876, some 3,000 Teton Sioux and Northern Cheyenne braves had also assembled in a vast encampment in the valley of the Little Bighorn, Montana.

Sitting Bull, a noted mystic and medicine man, subjected himself to the ordeal of the sacred Sun Dance so that he might obtain a vision of what lay ahead for his people. He was rewarded with a vision of many white soldiers falling, upside down, from the sky into his camp. And indeed, according to the prediction, the flamboyant General George Armstrong Custer and his US Seventh Cavalry rode to disaster. Custer and about 225 troopers were overwhelmed at the battle of the Little Bighorn, where Crazy Horse, the great Sioux chief, led his war-painted warriors into action with the battle-cry: "Today is a good day to fight! Today is a good day to die!"

Although a sensational Indian victory, Little Bighorn brought relentless retaliation from the white man. The Sioux nation was broken up and both Crazy Horse and Sitting Bull were killed. Today, the once-mighty Sioux live mainly on reservations in North and South Dakota. They, more than any other tribe, have stamped their identity on the American nation. Chief Iron Tail posed for the Indian head that adorned the nickel coin. Such pride, however, has been undermined by the constant legal struggle of the Sioux to claim back their cherished Black Hills, stolen from them by Custer and gold miners in the 1870s. With their fabulous deposits of uranium and gold, the Black Hills are now worth 50 billion dollars, and Indian leaders want these mineral riches to provide their people with work and a dignified life style.

For centuries before the white man came, the Indians roamed and hunted on the plains of America. But they did so on foot. It was the Spanish conquistadors who introduced the horse to their country. Many of the animals escaped into the wild, where their numbers multiplied. The Plains Indians tamed the wild mustangs and by the end of the eighteenth century all the tribes were mounted. All of the Indians tended to be splendid horsemen, but it was the Comanches who were acknowledged as the very best. George Catlin, the famous pioneer artist who lived among the Indians in the 1830s, praised their equestrian skill: "The Comanches are the most extraordinary horsemen that I have seen in all my travels. A Comanche on his feet is out of his element, and almost as awkward as a monkey on the ground without a limb or branch to cling to. But the moment he lays his hand upon a horse,

Opposite above
Brave Chief of the Pawnee tribe painted by
George Catlin in the 1830s. The painted hands
indicate victory over an enemy in close combat.

Opposite below
The Game of the Arrows as played by the
Mandans of the Upper Missouri. They competed
to see who could get the greatest number of
arrows flying in the air at one time. Painted by
George Catlin.

Below
Big Elk of the Omaha tribe, another fine study by
George Catlin. The warrior's black painted face
indicates he has recently killed an enemy.

Right
Navajo Indian Woman weaving a rug on a reservation in Arizona. Navajo women weave their traditional patterns almost perfectly but usually leave at least one small flaw, since perfection, they believe, is a quality reserved for the gods.

Below
Navajo hogan made from timber and brush. One half of a stereograph taken around 1900.

his face even becomes handsome, and he gracefully flies away like a different being."

George Catlin also described the favorite combat trick of the Comanche horseman, who would drop his body along the side of his galloping horse, "with his heel hanging over the horse's back, by which means he has the power of throwing himself up again, and changing to the other side of his horse if necessary. He will hang whilst his horse is at fullest speed, carrying with him his bow and shield, and also his long lance." Thus a warrior hid himself from enemy weapons.

An offshoot of the Shoshoni tribe of Wyoming, the Comanches were nomadic buffalo hunters who roamed the southwestern plains of Texas and New Mexico. For over a century, the Comanches waged war against the Spanish of Mexico and then the Texans, who dispossessed them of their best hunting grounds. They particularly hated the white buffalo hunters who wiped out entire herds to obtain their hides, leaving the meat to rot on the plains.

Allied with the Kiowas and the Apaches, the Comanches fought a bloody war against the Texans in 1874. Eventually, they were surrounded in their camp by the US Fourth Cavalry and slaughtered. Their chief, Quanah, declared that "I can learn the white man's way of life" and became a prosperous businessman with a large house in the Indian Territory of Oklahoma, where the Comanche reservation is today.

The Apaches took longer to subdue. These, the most feared of the Indians of the Southwest, were led by Geronimo. During the 1880s, he and his outlaw band plagued the frontier settlements of Arizona and Mexico. For two years, he was persuaded to return to the reservation. But Geronimo was restless and resumed his roaming and raiding. He twisted and turned to escape the relentless US troops with their Apache scouts. He could not run forever; in 1886 he surrendered and immediately became a celebrity. As one of the last defiant Indian warriors, he allowed himself to be exhibited at the 1904 World's Fair in St Louis, signing photographs of himself for 50 cents.

Captain Bourke of the US Third Cavalry summed up the notorious toughness of the Apache warrior: "His muscles are as hard as stone. I have seen one strike a match on the sole of his naked foot. The Apache has few wants and cares for no luxuries. War is his business, his life, and victory his dream". Today, most members of the various Apache tribes live on reservations in Arizona and New Mexico. They are accomplished cattlemen and their stock now ranks among the best. The Navajos, close relatives of the Apaches, live on the largest reservation in the US and are famous for their magnificent weaving and silverwork.

Right
A scene of intertribal warfare on the Plains, from a painting by Charles Schreyvogel. Tribes fought each other for hunting grounds, horses, and martial honor and esteem.

Not all Indians fought against the white man. Washakie, a prominent chief of the Shoshoni, realized early the futility of resisting the white settlers and the advantages to be gained from siding with them. He gave help to the settlers and 9,000 white pioneers signed a testimony to his kindness. In 1868, he secured for his people a reservation of their own choice, the desirable Wind River Valley of Wyoming. For his services with the US army in the Sioux War, Washakie was presented with an expensive saddle from the President. When the old chief died in 1900 at Fort Washakie in Wyoming, he was buried with full military honors. His people still live in the Wind River country.

Indians today earn their livelihood in many ways. A few reservations receive income from mineral deposits beneath their land. The Navajos realize a considerable amount from oil and uranium royalties, as well as oil and gas rentals. The Pueblos of New Mexico sit upon rich deposits of sand and gravel and receive substantial royalties from uranium, oil and gas. These payments are divided among the tribe and provide capital for investment in the potential of their land. The Apaches operate sawmills and derive much income from their forests. Some tribes have transformed areas of their beautiful land into popular recreation centers.

Oklahoma, once called Indian Territory, is the home of 67 tribes. In this melting pot, pride in Indian culture runs high. Sequoyah State Park is named after the Cherokee Indian leader who devised an alphabet for the Cherokee language. His cabin is preserved in Salisaw. There are many Indian festivals held throughout the state, but the most important is the annual American Indian Exposition, staged at Anadarko in August. The town also houses the permanent exhibits of the American Indian Hall of Fame, the Southern Plains Indian Exhibit and Craft Center, and Indian City USA, a recreated settlement of authentic Plains Indians huts and dwellings. Oklahoma has also been the center of a school of Indian painters, famous for their modern interpretations of old Indian themes. Indian culture is an ever-present reminder of their role in the country's history as "The First Americans".

Below
Navajo weavers, Susie Yazzi and Effie Holiday, work their loom in Monument Valley. This type of loom, adapted from the Pueblos, has been in use for centuries.

Right
Comanche Indians entertain visitors to their Oklahoma reservation with traditional dances.

Left
Anasazi Village in Mesa Verde National Park, Colorado. Anasazi means "ancient ones" and was the Indian name for the inhabitants of these remarkable stone apartment blocks eight hundred years ago.

Right
A Comanche in full panoply of feathers. Costumed dancers such as this make the annual American Indian Exposition at Anadarko, Oklahoma, a visual treat for visitors.

Opposite above
Taos Pueblo in New Mexico. Constructed of sun-dried clay bricks, adobe houses are still lived in today. The word adobe comes from the Spanish "adobar" meaning "to plaster". To make the bricks, wet clay is mixed with straw or grass.

Opposite below
A Navajo mother teaches her daughter how to use a loom. Such craft work is an ever-present link with an older culture that has survived the coming of the white man.

Previous page
Interior of a Mandan lodge painted by Karl
Bodmer in 1839. The Mandans of the Upper
Missouri were farmer-hunters who were always
friendly to the white man.

Above
"Watching the Wagon Train" by Oscar
Berninghaus. As the pioneers rolled westwards,
the Indians had to fight hard to keep their land.

Right
Hopi Indian rider at a rodeo in Arizona. Indians
are great cowboys and many tribes obtain a
substantial income from ranches and livestock.

Above
A Crow Indian in traditional regalia contemplates a tribal gathering on his reservation in Montana.

Left
Hopi Indian bull-riding in Arizona. Rodeos are now an important aspect of Indian life, providing an opportunity to test traditional skills of riding.

2. Wagons Moving West

"Go West, young man, and grow up with your country!" This phrase was made popular in the middle years of the last century by newspaper editor Horace Greeley, who knew that the future greatness of the United States lay in the development of the potentially rich wilderness that spread for around 2,000 miles west of the Mississippi River. And so countless adventurous young men and women from the eastern United States – and from all parts of the world – headed west in their wagons to colonize and plant the untilled land.

Key figures in the early exploration of the West were the "mountain men". Bearded and buckskinned, the hickory-hard fur trappers were the roughest, toughest frontiersmen of the pioneer period of the United States. In their constant search for untrapped beaver streams, they blazed trails across the Rocky Mountains and other high regions of the wilderness. Beaver fur was in great demand in the first half of the nineteenth century as it clad the stylish top hats of gentlemen in America and Europe. The trappers and traders came from Anglo-American, French and Spanish stock. They spoke a mixed tongue known as "mountain talk" and in dress, habits and general life style they differed little from the Indians they lived and fought with. Indeed, they have been called the "White Indians".

The most famous mountain men were John Colter, Hugh Glass, Grizzly Adams, Joe Meek, Jedediah Smith, Kit Carson and Jim Bridger. John Colter is credited with the discovery of the Teton Range and the South Pass of the Rocky Mountains, the Green River, the headwaters of the Snake, Pierre's Hole, Jackson's Hole and the area now embraced in Yellowstone National Park, Wyoming. Colter also won fame by surviving an incredible ordeal when captured by Blackfoot Indians in 1808. Having killed his companion, the Indians decided to give Colter a chance to live. Stripped of his clothing and moccasins, he was told to run for his life. Giving him a short head start, several hundred armed warriors dashed after the naked Colter, intent on hunting him down like a fleeing animal.

Colter showed the Indians what a mountain man was made of. He ran non-stop until the exertion caused blood to stream from his nose and mouth. His bare feet were ripped and bloodied by thorns and rocks, but still he ran on. Mile after mile, and one by one, he ran the pursuing Indians into the ground until only one remained at his heels. The heaving trapper stopped and faced the tenacious warrior, who threw his lance at the standing quarry. The spear landed at Colter's feet. He snatched the shaft from the ground and, as the Indian rushed him with upraised knife,

Opposite
Honeymoon trail wagon train in Arizona. Today many organizations recreate wagon trips along the rugged historical trails. It has also been used as a means of teaching juvenile delinquents the responsibility of working as a team.

Above
Modern mountain men enthusiasts gather at a meeting in Colorado. A world apart from the old annual "rendezvous" at which trappers met to sell their furs in a wild frenzy of drinking, gambling, and brawling.

Above left
Davy Crockett with his hunting dogs. Born in Tennessee, he became a hunter and army scout, Congressman and folk hero. He died at the Alamo in 1836 fighting for Texas independence.

Above right
Emigrants to the West halt on the long trail and settle down for the night. The hunter hands a brace of prairie chickens for the cooking pot.

Opposite below
Trappers resting on the trail, painted by Alfred Jacob Miller. Furs provided the basis of private and company fortunes, such as the Hudson Bay Company.

rammed the lance into the brave, killing him instantly. Colter struggled on for seven days until he reached the safety of a trading post.

Hugh Glass also demonstrated the toughness of the mountain men. He ran into an enraged grizzly bear while traveling with a small party of trappers. After a terrible struggle in which he managed to kill the bear with his knife, the horrifically injured Glass was more dead than alive. The leader of the expedition detailed two men to stay with him until he recovered or died. In the belief that Glass would never survive his awful wounds, the two men abandoned him, taking his rifle and equipment, and reported him dead and buried.

Incredibly, Glass hung on to life. Alone in the wilderness, he regained some strength by eating wild berries and roots. Unable to walk because of his injuries, he began to crawl towards Fort Kiowa, over 100 miles away. Perhaps the vision of revenge kept him going, for he vowed to kill the men who had deserted him. Eventually, he was found by a band of Indians who tended his wounds and helped him reach the fort. But when he confronted the two sorry men to exact vengeance, Glass relented and forgave them. Having recovered his much-prized rifle, Hugh Glass went on to further adventures until he was killed in an Indian fight in 1833.

Joe Meek was known more for his humor than his endurance. He was one of the

founders of Oregon and mightily proud of the little settlements established by the pioneers in that land. When a young journalist asked the great mountain man what changes he had seen in Oregon, Joe looked up at the towering mass of Mount Hood and replied: "Well, son, when I first came to this country, Mount Hood was a hole in the ground!" Certainly, the trails of the fur trappers and traders opened up the Far West to later settlers. When the fur trade collapsed in the 1830s and 1840s, because of the scarcity of beavers due to over-trapping and the collapse in the fashion for beaver hats, their trading posts developed into towns and cities. Many mountain men served as guides for the wagon trains that brought land-hungry settlers.

The most famous emigrant road was the Oregon Trail. In no way a proper highway, it was simply a series of parallel wagon ruts across the terrain, following rivers, forts and landmarks. Portions of the trail had existed for thousands of years as Indian footpaths connecting village to hunting ground. Along it, thousands of hopeful pioneers in ox-drawn covered wagons endured the 2,000 mile journey from Independence, Missouri, to the Oregon country, or branched off near the Great Salt Lake for California. This marathon trek involved countless hazards and hardships. It has been estimated that at least 30,000 men and women perished along the Oregon Trail up to 1859.

Above left
East of Leadville, Colorado, a group of abandoned mines and homes. From 1879 to 1885 the total product of Leadville mines in lead, silver, gold and other metals amounted to almost 100 million dollars.

Above right
An unfortunate hunter runs into an enraged grizzly bear. Only a rare few, such as trapper Hugh Glass, survived a close quarter encounter with this huge beast.

Left
One of a series of American Hunting Scenes published by Currier & Ives in the 1850s. The animal being hunted here is the elk, second largest in size of the American deer family, the moose being the biggest.

A typical pioneer wagon consisted of a rectangular wagon box about ten feet long with a canvas top cover, waterproofed with linseed oil. The four wheels were made of wood strengthened with iron. Few of the wagons had either springs or brakes. There was usually little room left inside a loaded wagon and so the settlers walked along beside their slow-moving vehicle.

The first wagon trains were organized along military lines. "One hundred men should be armed and equipped with a good rifle gun of large bore," advised the *Iowa Capitol Reporter* of 1843. "I would recommend that to 100 men, they elect one Captain, who should carry a spy glass, four Sergeants, four Corporals, and there ought to be a Bugler to give the signals. Guides and buffalo hunters will be required who will have to be paid a reasonable sum, as it will not do for everyone to go hunting and shooting at pleasure. Companies ought not to be less than 50 efficient fighting men, but 100 would be better. There are some Indians who are rather hostile and they might attack a small party for plunder."

A wagon train pulled by oxen, the preferred draft animal, averaged about ten miles a day. When the caravan halted at the day's end, the wagons were arranged in a circular or square compound which served as both corral for the animals and fortress against Indian attack. In good weather, the 2,000 mile trek could be made in five or six months.

The American frontier had never known a migration quite like that of the Mormons, a pioneer people bound together by the absolute authority of their Church and their formidable faith. Belonging to a new and unorthodox Christian religion, they were persecuted in the East and driven from place to place. Eventually their leader, Brigham Young, decided to lead his people to an isolated land far away. Where exactly, he did not know, but in 1847 the Mormon advance party set out. Instead of following the Oregon Trail, they blazed a new route to avoid trouble-making non-believers. Along the way, they encountered experienced frontiersmen. One of them, Jim Bridger, advised the Mormons not to settle in the arid Great Salt Lake region, but to push on to Oregon or California. "Why stop in that Godforsaken place?" he asked. "Nobody on earth would want it." To which Brigham Young replied: "If nobody on earth wants such a place, then that is the place for my people."

Immediately the Mormons began to irrigate, plant crops, build forts and cabins, explore and colonize thousands of square miles of virgin territory. They made the desert bloom. Salt Lake City was their Zion and state capital. Over the following decades tens of thousands of Mormon converts, many from Europe as well as the US, made the marathon journey to Utah. They came by covered wagon and on foot, pulling and pushing handcarts.

By the 1880s, all that remained unsettled of the West was the Indian Territory, a large tract of land which the government had reserved for the Indians and to which many tribes had been forced to move. In 1889, the Indians

Above
Salt Lake Valley from the hills above Salt Lake City, showing the State Capitol Building. "Why stop in that God-forsaken place?" Brigham Young was asked. "If nobody on earth wants such a place," he replied, "then that is the place for my people." The Mormons made Salt Lake City their Zion.

Left
Wolfe Ranch in Arches National Park, Utah. Wolfe was one of the first settlers in this beautiful region of rock spires and pinnacles. His cabin has remained as it was.

Right
Cultivating corn in Minnesota. A descendant of the first sod-busters who made a living for themselves in the Trans-Mississippi West.

were persuaded to sell two million acres of this territory and the Oklahoma District was thrown open to white settlement under the Homestead Act. This Act allowed a pioneer, on payment of a small fee, to claim 160 acres of public land. After living on and cultivating the land for five years, he received full title to the homestead.

When the Oklahoma District was opened up to homesteaders in 1889, it was done in the manner of a land rush. On the official signal to start, 100,000 eager settlers raced in from the border to stake their claim to 160 acres of America's last frontier. They rushed forward on horseback, and in buckboards and wagons, to obtain the best sites. By nightfall, the land was covered by tent towns. Six counties were born and the newly-founded Oklahoma City had a population of 10,000 tent dwellers. In 1907, the rest of the Indian Territory and Oklahoma entered the Union as the single state of Oklahoma.

The first transcontinental railroads enabled pioneers to travel more quickly and in greater comfort. But even with the coming of rail transportation, the wagon trains continued to roll westward. One railroad worker described seeing an emigrant caravan in Nebraska in the 1880s: "I could see an almost unbroken stream of emigrants from horizon to horizon, a distance of not less than eight miles or ten. Teams and covered wagons, some drawn by cows, horsemen, little bunches of cows, men walking, women and children riding. An endless stream of hardy, optimistic folk heading west to seek their fortunes and to settle an empire."

Today, you can trek into history by taking one of the "pioneer wagon train" trips organized by various vacation companies. One such outfit is Wagons Ho of Kansas. They offer covered wagon train trips of one to four days along 40 miles of the historic Smokey Hill Trail riding in an authentic wagon pulled by horse or mule teams. There are pioneer dresses and bonnets for the ladies. During overnight stops the wagons are formed into a circle, you eat campfire grub and sleep in tents. They even stage an Indian attack!

If you have an imaginative sense of history, taking such a trip is good for the soul. Following the original trail, hearing the creak of wagon wheels, the clop of hooves, passing natural landmarks seen by pioneer eyes more than a century ago, certainly evokes thoughts of those sturdy, persevering, courageous pilgrims who made the long, hazardous journey to settle the West.

Below
At Independence Day celebrations in Arizona, an old timer poses against a "prairie schooner". Such wagons carried a whole family's furniture, food supplies, cooking equipment, and water kegs.

Opposite
Oregon Trail wagon ruts at Ash Hollow, Nebraska. Over the years, since the great migration of 1843, thousands of emigrants wore a deeply rutted highway on their way West.

3. Gold Fever and Railroads

Denver, Colorado, high in the Rocky Mountains, is one of the most spectacular and stimulating of western cities, an exciting mixture of cultural sophistication, business dynamism and historical heritage. First it was gold that lured pioneers across the empty plains to the place that was to become Denver, then railroads and cattle.

The city was founded in 1858 at the start of the Pike's Peak gold rush. From a mining camp of a few tents it became a boom town with a population of 5,000. By the 1870s it was the major outfitting and banking center for the gold and silver prospectors of the region, which embraced Leadville, Georgetown, Central City and Cripple Creek. When Colorado achieved statehood in 1876, dynamic Denver became the capital.

Denver is proud of its golden roots. The dome of the State Capitol is covered with 24-carat gold leaf from Colorado mines. From the dome you get a panoramic view of the city, the Rocky Mountains and the Great Plains. Denver is called "The Mile High City" – the thirteenth step of the Capitol's west entrance is exactly one mile above sea level. The city houses the US Mint, which contains the largest depository of gold bullion outside Fort Knox. At one time Denver had a private mint which struck 10 and 20 dollar coins bearing an engraving of Pike's Peak, the mountain landmark for hopeful prospectors.

These seekers of gold and silver played a major role in winning the West. Whenever they "struck it rich", a rush to the area usually followed. Many mining camps faded quickly into ghost towns but some prospered into established townships and others developed into cities. Denver's roaring past is clearly evident in its preserved buildings, monuments and fascinating museums. The Molly Brown House, a restored mansion, is open to the public. Molly was born in a log cabin and married wealthy Johnny Brown of Denver. A remarkable woman and a survivor of the Titanic disaster of 1912 – she became known as "The Unsinkable Molly Brown" – her life has been immortalized in a musical and a movie.

In its early days Denver's backyard teemed with prospectors who panned the streams and dug the rocky slopes. In the first great strike, Central City was transformed from crude camp to boom town, renowned as the "richest square mile on earth". In its heyday Central City rivaled Denver in wealth and flamboyance. When President Grant visited the place in 1873 the front walk of the Teller House hotel (still there) was paved with solid silver bricks. Today, Central City is a popular tourist attraction. In nearby Golden, the Colorado Railroad Museum contains old steam locomotives and relics of narrow-gauge railroad days housed in a convertible train depot of the 1880s.

Opposite
Aspen, Colorado: once an old silver-mining town, now a top ski center and mecca for cultural events and festivals.

Above
A prospector in his mining cave home in Arizona. Prospectors' remote dwellings still provide shelter for present-day adventurers.

Left
Panning for gold. The simplest method of extracting gold, a prospector fills a wash pan with "pay dirt" and then swirls it around in the water, washing out the lighter sand and gravel to leave the heavier gold particles at the bottom.

Below
On the first transcontinental railroad; Amtrak has saved many of the rail-road passenger lines from extinction so that trains are now as much a part of the future of the West as its past.

Bottom
Reconstructed western town of Old Abilene, Kansas, where the Chisholm Trail ended.

Right
Panning for gold in California during the great rush that began in 1849. Between 1848 and 1852 the population of California increased from an estimated 15,000 to 250,000.

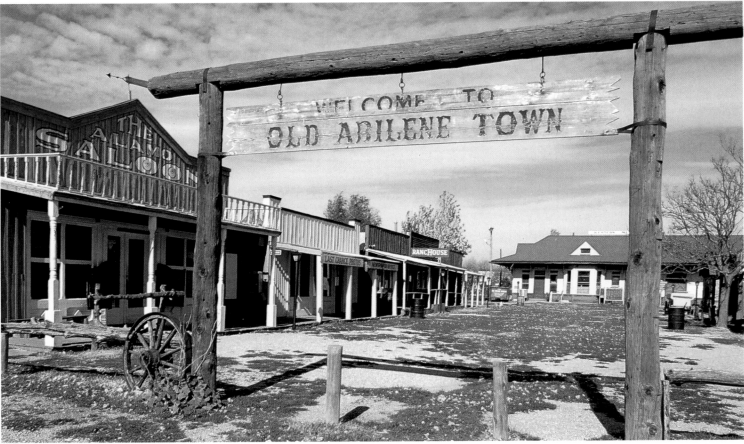

Just west of Colorado Springs is Cripple
Creek, a gold rush town still clothed in the
past, with buildings of lavish Victorian decor.
It has only 425 inhabitants and is still a mining
town. Visitors are allowed to descend 1,000
feet into the Mollie Kathleen Gold Mine.
Leadville, 120 miles southwest of Denver,
grew rich on silver-lead mines. Its most
celebrated citizen was Horace Tabor, a poor
prospector who struck it rich. His Matchless
Mine made him a silver millionaire and a
national figure. "Silver Dollar" Tabor, as he
was called, became Leadville's first mayor,
then the governor of Colorado, and eventually
a US senator. He built a grand opera house for
Leadville and later another for Denver. Tabor
lived high, wide and handsome and spent
millions. In the late 1880s he ran into
financial difficulties, his mines failed to
produce and other projects collapsed. When
the world price of silver dropped sharply in
1893, Tabor found himself broke. He died, as
he had started out, a poor man.

The town of Tombstone, Arizona, was
founded on a silver strike made by prospector
Ed Schieffelin in 1878. It was Apache country
and Schieffelin had been warned that all he
would find out there would be his tombstone –
so when he made his discovery he named the
resulting boom town Tombstone. The place is
famous as the scene of the "Gunfight at the
O.K. Corral" in which Wyatt Earp and his
brothers wiped out the Clanton-McLaury
gang in 1881. The mines became flooded in
the 1890s and Tombstone declined into a
ghost town. Now in restored condition and
publicized as the "Town Too Tough to Die," it
is a popular tourist attraction. Its annual
"Helldorado" celebration is climaxed by a
recreation of the shootout at the O.K. Corral.

Helena, state capital of Montana, was
founded on a gold strike. In 1864 John Cowan
was on the point of giving up his long, futile
search for gold when he decided to try one last
spot in the foothills of the Rockies. He named
the place Last Chance Gulch. He hit gold and
started a rush. A town began to grow and, as it
flourished on gold and silver, its solid citizens
decided to rename Last Chance Gulch with
the more dignified Helena. However, Last
Chance Gulch, site of the original gold strike,
remains the name of the city's main street.

Virginia City, Montana, presents an
authentic recreation of frontier living. More
than 20 buildings have been reconstructed and
restored to give visitors an insight into the life
style of an Old West town. Gold discoveries in
and around this town netted 300 million
dollars, and the last mining operations only
ended in 1937. There is another Virginia City
in Nevada, once the largest mining town in
the state. Founded in 1859 on the fabulous
Comstock Lode, its mines produced some
400 million dollars in silver and gold. By
1890 the mines became unworkable and
Virginia City became a ghost town. Today,
this restored historic town enjoys a new boom
period, with half a million tourists visiting the
place annually.

The great California Gold Rush
transformed the little settlement in San
Francisco Bay – population 459 in 1847 – into
one of the world's busiest ports. By 1852 the

Above
Prospectors bring their gold dust to a Denver
bank in the 1860s. When Colorado achieved
statehood in 1876, gold-rich Denver became the
capital city.

Below
Denver insurance building, Colorado. The mile-
high city has always been wealthy. In 1896, the
dome of the State Capitol was covered with gold
leaf costing nearly 200,000 dollars.

Right
The ghost town of Bodie, California. Gold and
silver brought prosperity to the West but
frequently when the mines ran out, the
community broke down and towns were left as
empty shells.

population had risen to 35,000. The mass migration to California began in 1849 – hence the term "forty-niner" for a prospector – and lasted several years. The man who triggered the great stampede was not a prospector but a carpenter named John Marshall, and he discovered gold quite by chance.

In January 1848 Marshall was engaged in building a sawmill for landowner John A. Sutter. The sawmill was sited at Coloma on the south fork of the American River, some 50 miles from Sutter's Fort, where the city of Sacramento now stands. Marshall was attracted by something glittering in the waters of the millrace, and picked up several small nuggets of gold. He reported his find to John Sutter, who wanted the discovery kept secret, for he realized that a rush of gold seekers to the area would ruin his flourishing estate. He was absolutely right. When the hot news leaked out and the human flood swamped Coloma, Sutter's property was trampled and vandalized and he died in poverty. So did Marshall, who never made a dollar out of his historic discovery.

By 1852 more than 250,000 prospectors and settlers, from all parts of the world, had poured into California seeking gold and a better life. The lure of the golden state, blessed as it is with a splendid climate, fertile land and mineral wealth, continues to attract the enterprizing and the dreamers.

At Sacramento, the state capital, which grew up around Sutter's Fort, you can see a reconstruction of the original settlement. In January 1863 Sacramento witnessed the beginning of an enormous engineering project that would hasten the settlement and development of the western lands – the first transcontinental railroad linking the Atlantic Ocean to the Pacific. Two companies built the railroad: the Central Pacific drove east from Sacramento, and the Union Pacific pushed west from Omaha, Nebraska. The two tracks eventually joined at a spot called Promontory in Utah. A railroad already existed across the eastern states to Omaha. Central Pacific broke ground first at Sacramento and Union Pacific started work in December 1863.

Progress was delayed by financial problems and the Civil War, and work did not get properly underway until the end of the conflict in 1865. From then on until its completion, the building of the Pacific railroad dominated the national interest. It was the biggest engineering project America had ever known, hailed as the "Eighth Wonder of the Modern World". The UP line was largely built by gangs of Irish immigrants and ex-soldiers. CP found it difficult to get enough white workers and brought in shiploads of laborers from China. By 1868 there were 11,000 Chinese working on this railroad and high tribute was paid to these industrious Orientals by Leland Stanford, president of CP. "Without the Chinese," he said, "it would have been impossible to complete the western portion of this national highway."

After covering 1,775 miles between them the two railroads joined at Promontory, a desolate desert spot north of Great Salt Lake. The marriage between east and west was

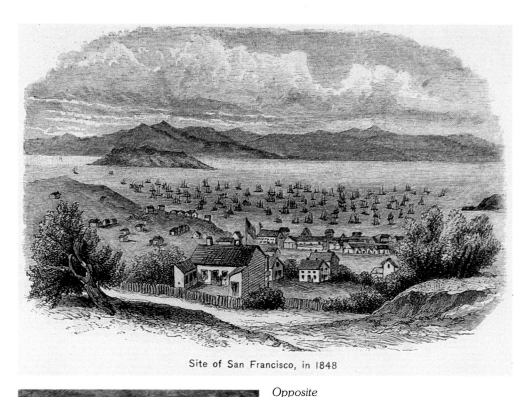

Site of San Francisco, in 1848

H. A. W. TABOR.

Opposite
The Transamerica Pyramid, San Francisco. The great California Gold Rush transformed a little settlement of 459 people in 1847 into the financial and insurance capital of the West.

Above
The little community of San Francisco in 1848, the year in which gold was found at Coloma.

Center
John A. Sutter painted by Frank Buchser in 1866. It was the gold found on Sutter's land that sparked off the great rush to California in 1849.

Below
Horace Tabor, the silver king of Leadville, Colorado. Starting out poor he struck it rich, amassing great wealth; but things went wrong and he died poor.

sealed by the ceremony of the Golden Spike on May 10, 1869, in which top officials of both companies tapped in the last spike – made of gold – to mark properly the historic occasion. The gold spike was removed after the ceremony, replaced with a normal one, and rests today in the Stanford University Museum at Palo Alto, California. The first transcontinental railroad heralded the coming greatness of the United States, opening up the vast interior wilderness to development that made the nation the richest and most powerful in the modern world.

The Union Pacific grew into one of America's major, most enduring railroad systems. The Central Pacific lost its separate identity in 1885 when it was absorbed by the Southern Pacific Railroad. Completion of the Northern Pacific Railroad in 1883 marked the first through route from Lake Superior over the northern plains to the Pacific coast. By widely advertising and promoting its federal land grants at home and in Europe, and transporting immigrants across the nation, the Northern Pacific also contributed greatly to the settling of the West, as did other railroads.

There are still many relics of steam train days to be seen all over the country. A number of antique locomotives have been restored to their former smoke-belching glory and now haul trains packed with tourists over special scenic routes. But the great days of railroad travel have gone, possibly forever. With air and road travel dominating the passenger service, the railroads declined in importance and prestige and became mainly functional freight carriers. A number went out of business.

In 1971 the federal government created Amtrak, which took over all passenger operations of the old railroad companies and kept them running despite the need for huge subsidies. There are many who hold the opinion that trains represent the future and not the past in transportation in America. The high price of gas and new labor agreements could well herald a renaissance of the passenger train. After all, there is no better way to view and enjoy the varied, breathtaking scenery of the western states.

Below
Picture showing the construction of the Central Pacific Railroad. Shortage of white laborers caused the company to ship in thousands of Chinese coolies, who proved excellent workers. Indeed, it was said that the great engineering project would not have been completed but for the Chinese.

Left
Skiing has become a great dollar earner for mountain resorts: the Winterskol Festival at Aspen, Colorado.

Below
A tourist train on the Cumbres & Toltec Scenic Railroad which runs between Antonito in Colorado and Chama in New Mexico. The beauty of the colors at fall attract thousands of visitors to the railroad which reaches 10,022 feet.

Opposite
The old cabin on the Plains: a ghost town near St. George, Utah.

Left
Old wagon wheels in a ghost town near Cody, Wyoming. Deserted by prospectors, these get-rich-quick settlements are now an eerie reminder of the Old West.

Below
Golden Gate Bridge, San Francisco. Drive across the bridge from Downtown and you capture a little of the old timber-built character of the former fishing community at Sausalito.

4. Cowboys and Cattle Barons

A working cowboy of today is a very different *hombre* to the cowboy of a century ago. The development of the western cattle industry and modern technology has changed the cowboy's work pattern, his philosophy, aspirations and lifestyle. Cowboys still ride the range in Texas, Wyoming, Montana, Arizona, Nevada and other states. But a pickup truck or jeep is just as important and often more practical than a cow pony. Helicopters are also employed to monitor scattered cattle. A good mechanic is vital to the success of a modern ranch, and a top tool hand is harder to find – and keep – than a top rider.

It seems the cowboy is a dying breed. In Wyoming, "The Cowboy State", the number of ranch hands has declined from 6,000 to 4,000 over the past five years. It is not difficult to understand why. In Wyoming, for example, a young cowhand can go to the nearest oil field or coal mine and get a decent job for more money. The average weekly pay in the oil or coal industry is more than triple that paid to the ordinary cowpoke. The same situation prevails in Texas and Arizona.

"Most of the cowboys I ever knew are long dead," opined a veteran ranch boss. "There ain't no point in a young fella learning to be a top hand when he can make so much more doing an easier job."

Despite the social changes, the cowboy continues to be necessary to cattle ranching. His long working day has no set hours. "When the job needs to be done," said a Nevada ranch hand, "it gets done." And his jobs are varied – from repairing and oiling pumps and engines, mending fences and shoeing horses to the traditional tasks of roping and branding calves. His winter duties include breaking ice on water holes and pitching feed to cattle from the back of a truck.

The cowboy has changed and so have the cattle. The crossbreed, docile, beef-heavy creature of today in no way compares with the lean, half-wild, fast-moving Longhorn of days gone by – the legendary Texas Longhorn from which the modern cattle industry grew and prospered. The cowboy and the Longhorn rode into history together.

The cowboy originated in Texas in the middle of the last century. His methods of handling cattle on horseback, his colorful and practical work clothes, his leather equipment, were inherited and adapted from the *vaquero*, the Spanish-Mexican cowboy who predated the Texas type. Texas was the land of the hardy, feral Longhorn, which had descended

Texas cattle being loaded into railroad cars at Abilene, Kansas, in the 1870s, for transportation east. Abilene was the first of the rowdy railhead cow towns.

Jared L. Brush.

Charles Lux.

R. G. Head.

John H. Iliff.

Thos. H. Lawrence.

John W. Snyder.

John T. Lytle.

from cattle first brought over by the Spanish in the seventeenth century. During the Civil War the Longhorns, left untended, reproduced themselves in great numbers. With the war over, Texan ex-soldiers returned to an impoverished country teeming with some six million Longhorns.

The northern states were hungry for beef and Texas was eager and ready to supply it. So began the period of the long cattle drives and the hard-riding Texas cowboy became a national figure. The Longhorns were driven up from Texas over dusty trails to railhead cattle towns in Kansas – Abilene, Dodge City, Wichita, Newton – and there loaded into railroad cars and taken east for slaughter and marketing. From 1866 to 1895 some ten million cattle were driven up from Texas to railhead cowtowns, or to stock new ranges on the central and northern plains.

At trail's end the free-spending cowboys kicked up a shindy with their drinking, gambling and fighting, so the cattle towns hired noted gunfighters to control the rowdy Texans and the rough element they attracted. Wyatt Earp, Bat Masterson and Wild Bill Hickock were among the marshals and lawmen who rose to fame as peacekeepers of the cattle towns. Abilene boomed as a railhead depot from 1867 to 1872 when its law-abiding citizens, weary of the troublesome cattle trade, requested the Texans to drive their herds elsewhere.

Abilene continued to prosper as an agricultural center. Its most famous son was president Dwight D. Eisenhower, Texas-born but reared and buried in Abilene. Today, a visitor can see a number of reminders and images of its roaring cowboy days. Old Abilene Town is an authentic reconstruction of the place during its cattle boom period. A boulder on the post office lawn marks the end of the celebrated Chisholm Trail. In the Abilene Cemetery is a stone marking the grave of Marshal Tom Smith, a noted peace officer killed while upholding the law in 1870.

Dodge City also attracts tourists with a recreation of historic Front Street with its Long Branch Saloon, a haunt of Wyatt Earp. Wichita has grown from primitive cow town to the largest city in Kansas, a major center of aircraft production. The city acknowledges its beginnings with a reconstruction of Cow Town, a replica of Wichita in 1872.

Cattle ranching spread north and west from Texas to Wyoming, Montana, the Dakotas, New Mexico, Colorado and Arizona. The open range cattle industry dominated the Great Plains from 1870 to 1885. It declined in importance for a number of reasons: overstocked ranges, a fall in beef prices and a wicked winter that wiped out herds on the open range. Then encroaching farmers and their barbed wire, and the spreading railroads, ended the period of the free open range.

The Longhorn, once numbering millions, began to disappear from the ranges in the 1880s with the introduction of improved beef cattle – the Shorthorn and Hereford for greater meat production, the Brahman for its resistance to Texas tick fever. By 1900 intensive cross-breeding had nearly erased the typical Longhorn, and by 1920 it was clear

Opposite
A gallery of cattle kings. They made immense fortunes from raising cattle on the free grass of the open range. The cattle industry dominated the Great Plains from 1870 to 1885.

Below
Working cowboys in Wyoming. Some dude ranches allow tourists to follow cowboys on a real round-up. At the end of the day you sleep on your own bed-roll out on the prairie.

Above
Cowboys roping a steer, a painting by Charles M. Russell, an ex-cowboy from Montana who became one of the nation's foremost artist historians of the Old West. Russell died in 1926 and today his paintings command high prices in the art world.

that prompt action by government and private endeavor was necessary to save the Longhorn from extinction.

Small herds of Longhorns were settled on wildlife reserves. The first annual meeting of the Texas Longhorn Breeders Association was held in Lawton, Oklahoma, in 1964. This organization keeps a register of the animals, records their ancestry and preserves the breed undiluted. Recent surveys show that some 5,000 Longhorns remain in the US. Of these, about 600 are on federal refuges, the rest in state or private herds and in zoos and parks. Thankfully, the Longhorn – a living link with the old cattle drives – is now safe from extinction. The buffalo was saved for posterity in a similar manner.

The plutocrats of the plains were the so-called cattle kings or barons – pioneers who claimed, purchased or just assumed ownership by occupation of vast tracts of grazing land and raised great herds of cattle. Tough and ruthless, they held their domains by force of arms: there was John Chisum of New Mexico, who owned some 100,000 head; Granville Stuart of Montana, who greatly reduced the cattle rustlers in that territory by summarily lynching them. His vigilantes were known as "Stuart's Stranglers". Of all the celebrated cattle kings, Richard King of Texas was the most aptly named.

Born in New York in 1825, Richard King went to sea at 13 as a cabin boy. In Texas in 1847 he bought a small steamer and traded on the Rio Grande. In a few years he owned 20 steamboats and decided, in 1852, that he wanted a cattle ranch and purchased 75,000 acres, in Nueces County on the coastal plain, from the holders of the original Spanish land grants. He erected a stockade and fort armed with a cannon and fought off Indians and Mexican bandits. By the time he died in 1885, King's domain encompassed 600,000 acres containing 100,000 cattle and 10,000 horses.

The King Ranch today is the largest in the nation with holdings of some 823,000 acres spreading over Nueces, Kenedy, Kleberg and Willacy counties. It has made available to the public a 12-mile loop that leads past its headquarters, stables and other points of interest. It was this ranch that introduced the Santa Gertrudis breed of cattle – an American original. The development of the Santa Gertrudis breed dates back to the early 1900s when the King Ranch recognized the inability of Hereford and Shorthorn cattle to produce profitably under the adverse environmental conditions of south Texas. In 1910 it was decided to crossbreed with Brahman, renowned for its hardiness. The Shorthorn and Brahman mixture proved most productive.

In 1940 the US Department of Agriculture recognized the Santa Gertrudis as America's first beef breed. The Santa Gertrudis Breeders International was incorporated in April 1951 to standardize and certify those

animals designated as "purebred" and to establish rigorous controls for grading-up to purebred herds. Why the name Santa Gertrudis? It was the name of the Spanish land grant where Richard King first established his ranch. Today, the hardy pest-and-disease-resistant Santa Gertrudis breed can be found in 41 American states, Canada, Mexico, Central and South America, Europe, Africa, Australia, Southeast Asia and the Soviet Union.

The spirit of the hard-riding cowboy is kept alive and kicking by rodeo – big money sport attended by more than ten million spectators annually. The word "rodeo" comes from the Spanish *rodear* meaning "round-up". The sport originated among the old-time cowboys who competed with each other in riding bucking horses and roping cattle. Rodeo entered big league sport in 1936 when the present Rodeo Cowboys Association was formed. Today, this body sanctions over 500 professional shows throughout the year in the US and Canada, offering prize money totalling millions of dollars.

Top riders travel all over North America to compete. There are six standard events: saddle bronc riding, bareback bronc riding, bull riding, steer wrestling, calf and team roping. In the saddle bronc contest the rider must stay in the bouncing saddle for ten seconds, in bareback bronc and bull riding he must stay on the animal for eight seconds. The rider must not only stay the distance but do so with great style according to a number of strict rules. The big prize money makes the sport highly competitive. The rider who wins the most prize money in the season is named World Champion All-Around Cowboy. A number of cowboys, once ordinary ranch hands, have won fame and fortune riding in the rodeo.

Left
A modern cattle drive in Arizona. Cowboys today are more likely seen in a pickup truck than riding a mustang.

Above right
Showing the flag. A cowboy proudly carries the stars and stripes at a rodeo in Jackson, Wyoming

Below right
Working cowboys and cattlemen relax on a ranch near Jackson, Wyoming.

Previous page
Saddle bronc riding at a rodeo in Wyoming. In this event the contestant must hold the reins with one hand only and stay in the saddle for ten seconds – with great style.

Right
The Texas Longhorn, the hardy crittur on which the cattle industry was founded. Crossbreeding and the introduction of better beef animals brought the Longhorn to near extinction.

Below
A cowhand and his horse. The number of cowboys is ever declining. Most young men prefer the higher wages paid by the oil industry.

Opposite
Westerners cooking up a storm. A favorite dish of old-time cowboys was "son-of-a-bitch" stew which contained almost anything. A great delicacy was the broiled testicles of a steer, which cowboys called "prairie oysters".

A Westerner takes it easy outside a Pawn Shop on the corner in Old Tucson, Arizona. In actual fact the "authentic" scene is bogus, for Old Tucson is a converted movie set.

MAC-MILLAN
PAWN SHOP
FARM-LOANS CA

HAND
ES

WENT TO TOMBSTONE.
VISIT AND TRADE AT
THE "GENERAL
STORE" —THANK YOU

ALL KINDS OF ITEMS
FOR TOWN AND RANCH
PELTS, FURS,
BELTS AND SPURS
SUITS AND HATS
DRESS AND WORK
BOOTS IN MOST SIZES
TRAPS FOR ALL
SIZE OF GAME
CHOICE RIFLES, HAND
GUNS, NEW AND USED.
CARTRIDGES
"MAC MILLAN WILL
FIX YOU UP RIGHT"

$100
"PHAETON"

W. L. DOUGLAS
$3 SHOE

PAWN AND BUY
TRADE FOR QUALITY

GET THE MOST FOR
YOUR MONEY HERE
CASH LOANS FOR THE
WORKING FARMER

A FAIR DEAL
EVERY TIME

WE AIM TO SATISFY

NO REFUNDS

OATS

5. They spell it O-I-L

There is an old saying that "Other states were made or born, Texas grew from hide and horn." Texas, "The Lone Star State", cradle of the cattle industry and a major producer of beef, also provides one-third of the nation's oil production. The petroleum industry has brought Texas immense wealth, economic power and political influence. Its continuing prosperity is reflected in its major cities, growing bigger and more impressive with each new steel and tinted glass skyscraper.

Texas first tapped its oil treasure at about the same time that the internal combustion engine was developed. The automobile changed the American way of life as no other machine has yet done. Texas is so vast that, to its inhabitants, a car is like wings to a bird. Petroleum makes the wheels of the world go round and Texas has great reserves of oil as yet untapped.

The discovery of oil started a new Wild West. As black gold gushed forth in Texas, Oklahoma, Wyoming, Montana and California, boom towns sprang up overnight, attracting the usual frontier riffraff. Lawlessness prevailed. In 1924 the upright citizens of Cromwell, Oklahoma, approached the renowned peace officer Bill Tilghman to serve as marshal and restore law and order. Tilghman, a former marshal of Dodge City, Kansas, was over 70 at the time and retired. Nevertheless he accepted the post and was doing a good job until one night, trying to disarm a drunk, he was shot dead. A veteran of the Old West had fallen victim to the new Wild West. In other boom towns martial law had to be imposed.

The first mention of oil in the US is contained in a letter penned in 1759 from the commandant of Fort Duquesne to General Montcalm. In it, the writer describes a religious ceremony of the Seneca Indians on the Venango River: "The surface of the stream was covered with thick black scum which, upon applying a torch at a given signal, burst into complete conflagration." Before the oil boom, petroleum was used to burn in lamps. Until the development of new methods of refining crude, only two products, coal oil and axle grease, were produced in quantity.

The story of the modern economic power of petroleum begins with the drilling of Drake's Well in a wild part of Pennsylvania in 1859. The first oil well produced 20 to 30 barrels a day. This success started the first oil rush and Oil Creek Valley, Pennsylvania, suddenly sprouted a forest of timber derricks drilling for the new liquid gold. From Pennsylvania the oil industry swept across the nation. Ohio and West Virginia had booms similar to that of Oil Creek. Then the West and Southwest became the center of the industry.

Fortunes were made overnight in those early days of oil discovery and many towns and cities have grown from oil strikes. Men

COLONEL E. L. DRAKE.

Opposite
Oklahoma is a major producer of petroleum. There are even oil-producing wells in the grounds of the Capitol building, Oklahoma City, as the cover of this brochure proudly displays.

Left
Edwin L. Drake, who supervised the drilling of America's first oil-producing well in western Pennsylvania in 1859.

Below
Drake's Well, a primitive timber derrick that housed the drill which started an oil-boom rush to the region. This first well produced 20 to 30 barrels a day.

THE DRAKE WELL.

A man called six times to give Mr. Rockefeller a cure for dyspepsia. But John D. knows what he needs.

Right
John D. Rockefeller made his multi-millions by dominating the oil business in the United States, as this cartoon of 1903 makes clear.

Below
This Pierce-Arrow car advertisement of 1911 symbolizes the end of the Old West. The coming of the car brought prosperity and easy mobility to millions of Americans. Petroleum and the automobile changed the West.

Opposite
Cathedral of Glass, Los Angeles, California. The hard-edge of Californian high-tech built upon the low-tech of the 'forty-niners.

who developed the industry became outstanding figures in commerce, the most celebrated being John D. Rockefeller. Starting his working life as a clerk in a merchant's house, he turned his attention to the oil business and, in 1865, established the Standard Oil plant at Cleveland, Ohio. Five years later the Standard Oil Company was incorporated with John D. Rockefeller as president. By 1881 the company's interests were so wide and its profits so extensive that the whole was formed into the Standard Oil Trust. Although the courts sought to break the Standard Oil monopoly, Rockefeller's organization continued to dominate the industry in America. John D. amassed a fabulous family fortune from nature's gift to the modern world, but he and his descendants have given many millions of dollars to charity, universities and research foundations for the benefit of fellow Americans.

In Oklahoma, oil and gas are produced in 71 of the state's 77 counties. The oil industry here was established during the boom years of 1912-29. Oklahoma's Capitol is unique among government buildings – it has an oil well underneath it. To bring up the oil located beneath the building, Capitol Site No 1 was completed in 1942. The derrick stands 431 feet from the center of the building in what was once a flower bed. This well, and the other producing wells on the Capitol's grounds, have generated millions of dollars in state revenue since they were drilled.

Wyoming's petroleum and coal industries are the largest employers in the state. Known as "The Cowboy State", the ranch hand population of Wyoming is decreasing as cowboys leave the range for the better pay available in oil fields and coal mines. Despite the pervading influence of modern technology, the streets of Wyoming's towns and cities are full of guys and girls in cowboy boots and hats. A visitor is well aware he's in the heart of the West. Casper is an oil boom city that boasts 40 millionaires in a population of some 40,000.

The construction of a refinery for the California Star Oil Company in the 1870s marked the start of the oil industry in the West, for it predated by a number of years similar developments in Texas, Oklahoma and Montana. By 1885 California's annual production of crude oil had reached 500,000 barrels. The first oil well in Texas was drilled by L. T. Barret in September 1866 at Oil Springs, Nacogdoches County. It produced ten barrels a day. There is a memorial to L. T. Barret on the campus of Stephen F. Austin State University, and the site of the first well has been restored and is open to the public.

The Texas oil boom literally blew in at 10 am on January 10, 1901 with a gusher drilled by A. F. Lucas at Spindletop, near the little settlement of Beaumont, which became a boom town overnight. The Spindletop gusher transformed the oil industry, producing several thousand times more oil than any previous well. Other derricks sprang up around the Lucas well, refineries were built and pipelines laid. Beaumont flourished with the flowing oil and is today an industrial giant, a major port and agricultural center. Its

The Pierce-Arrow

lusty beginnings can be viewed in the recreation of Gladys City-Spindletop Boomtown with buildings and equipment of the period, and the Lucas Gusher Monument.

After Spindletop, gusher followed gusher in Texas. Ranger was a quiet rural community founded in the 1870s near a Texas Ranger camp. In October 1917 a gusher – McClesky No 1 – blew in and started a stampede. Due to the First World War, demand for oil was at an all-time high, and the lure of instant riches brought a rush of humanity to Ranger. Within a year the population exploded from 1,000 to 30,000. Small farmers became millionaires. Four railroads raced to complete lines to the town. As in many cases the boom was short-lived. Today, Ranger has a population of some 3,000. There is still oil activity but farming and ranching are the major interests. A granite monument marks the site of McClesky No 1.

The exciting stories of Beaumont and Ranger were duplicated many times in Texas during the ensuing years. Iraan came into existence with an oil strike in 1928; its name combines those of the townsite owners, Ira and Ann Yates. That gusher remains one of the largest producing oil wells in North America. In 1930 the great East Texas Oil Field was discovered, which once numbered some 26,000 producing wells and covered 130,000 acres, making it the largest field in

Texas. Between 1930 and 1964 these wells produced more than 3.6 billion barrels of oil, and the field still has about 18,000 producing wells.

Texans drill for black gold on land and in the Gulf of Mexico. There are two types of operators: the "majors", giant corporations such as Texaco, Exxon, Mobil and Gulf, and the independent "wildcat" outfits. A wildcatter is a gambler, for he will risk millions of dollars in drilling unproven ground. The old wildcatters often worked on instinct, though the modern variety consult geological reports and seek advice of other highly specialized scientists.

Of all the major cities in Texas, Houston and Dallas in particular reflect the enormous wealth and vitality generated by the petroleum industry. Houston is the state's largest city, the so-called "Golden Buckle on the Sun Belt". Founded in 1836 this metropolis of one-and-half million is the financial center of the Texas oil business. It is one of the nation's greatest seaports and houses the headquarters of the Lyndon B. Johnson Space Center.

The late President Johnson was a good old Texas boy, born on a ranch near Johnson City, Blanco County, a settlement founded by his pioneer ancestors. When he was born in 1908 his paternal grandfather rode on horseback to his neighbors and proudly made the prophecy, "A United States senator was born this

Below
Downtown skyline, Dallas, Texas. The oil boom brought as many people to the West and founded as many cities as did the Gold Rush. Dallas is the banking and business center of the South West.

Opposite
An oilman handles a pipe ninety feet above drilling floor on an offshore rig. Today the really big oil strikes are being made in Alaska, the new West.

Opposite
Oil pumps on the Texan plains. In the early boom days pumps and derricks were sited close together in order to exploit a particular strike, making strange forests.

Upper
Tom Rafferty, Dallas versus Washington in the Dallas Center. The name Dallas Cowboys demonstrates that Texans are mighty proud of their cattle trade roots.

Lower
Oil tanker at Port Long Beach, California.

morning." Johnson worked hard to climb to the top of the political ladder. On his retirement from Presidential office he returned to the L.B.J. Ranch and lived as a cattleman until he died of a heart attack in 1973. His century-old boyhood home is open to the public.

Houston's skyline is constantly changing as new buildings rise – photographers have to update their views of the city every year. Astrodomain is a 100 million dollar entertainment complex that includes the celebrated Astrodome, the world's first air-conditioned domed stadium for baseball, football (home team the Houston Oilers), rodeo and other sports. It seats up to 66,000 with adjacent parking for 30,000 cars. Astrohall is one of the world's largest exhibition centers and home of the Houston Livestock Show and Rodeo, a rip-roaring annual event that kicks off with the arrival of up to 10,000 trail riders from Texas and Louisiana.

Dallas – "Big D" – second in size to Houston, is the banking and business center of the Southwest, home of more insurance companies than any other city in the nation. Its glass-sided, sun-flashing skyscrapers house 400 of America's largest industrial corporations. Dallas has more Cadillacs *per capita* than any other US city. Founded in 1841, and named after Vice-President George Mifflin Dallas, this frontier settlement benefited greatly from the arrival of several immigrations of skilled and cultured groups of French, German, English, Swiss and other Europeans. By the middle 1870s Dallas had developed into a thriving business town with a cosmopolitan urbanity unmatched anywhere on the frontier at that time.

Today, Dallasites pursue culture and sport with almost as much enthusiasm as business. Any day or night of the year there is an amazing variety of entertainment to choose from: opera, ballet, music, theater. When the Dallas Cowboys play football in the 65,000-seat Texas Stadium every seat is sold long beforehand. Fort Worth, close neighbor to Dallas, grew rich on beef and oil-related industries. The Dallas-Fort Worth Regional Airport is the largest in the US, but despite their partnership in the airport, the two cities have very different characters.

Will Rogers said that "Fort Worth is where the West begins and Dallas is where the East peters out." Fort Worth grew from a military post and after the Civil War became a major shipping and supply depot for cattlemen. Its stockyards rivaled Chicago's in size. It remained a cowboy town until the oil companies moved in during the 1920s. Today, Fort Worth is a manufacturing center and headquarters of many petroleum industries.

The city is proud of its pioneer past, which it celebrates with several festivals. The Chisholm Trail Round-Up in June offers an enjoyable series of parades, rodeos, street dances and mock shoot-outs. In September there are Pioneer Days, festivals staged in the historic Stockyards Area, where renovated stores, saloons and restaurants front traditional boardwalks in the style of the Old West.

Above left
Covered shopping mall in Houston, Texas.
Much of the wealth of Houston and Dallas is no
longer derived from oil alone but from business
in other fields.

Above right
Wheels across the West modern style. Once,
pioneers used uncomfortable wagons, now
travelers pile into luxurious mobile homes.

Left
Oil tanker transporting black gold. Petroleum
makes the wheels of the world go round and the
Lone Star State has great reserves of oil yet
untapped.

6. Unchanging Grandeur

Yellowstone in Wyoming is the oldest and largest national park in the United States. Amid its magnificent canyons and roaring waterfalls, visitors can enjoy the wonders and beauty of a wilderness untarnished by man. When mountain man Jim Bridger first talked of the hot springs and gushing geysers he had seen at Yellowstone, nobody believed him. One newspaper, previously interested in Bridger's travel stories, refused to publish these tall tales. Bridger called the wonderful landscape "the place where Hell bubbled up".

Overwhelmed by the natural spectacle, it was at Yellowstone that the early nation-makers realized that this primeval splendor must be treasured – a philosophy of conservation that has since spread all around the world. In 1872, President Grant signed into law an act creating the two million acres of Yellowstone National Park, the first national park in the world. It was an act of respect towards the remarkable scenery that greeted the nation's pioneers. Or, as one US Senator said in 1872, "We should show the world that they are wrong when they say that Americans are interested only in the almighty dollar."

So vast is Yellowstone National Park, nearly 3,500 square miles, that weeks on end are needed to explore its landscape. It has its own Grand Canyon, sheer cliffs rising over 1,000 feet above the Yellowstone river, and the Upper and Lower Falls, two beautiful cataracts plummeting a total of 417 feet. But most famous of all is the geyser called Old Faithful. One of thousands of hot springs dotted across the volcanic landscape, its name and fame derive from its regular eruptions. Bubbling up from thousands of feet below the ground, the boiling water bursts out at intervals varying between 33 and 96 minutes, reaching a height of 106 to 184 feet. There are bigger geysers in Yellowstone, but none so regular or so well known.

The disbelief with which early reports of Yellowstone were received is understandable. The stumps of redwood forests petrified beneath volcanic ash were exaggerated into a strange frozen world by the fur trappers that first saw them. They told of a land carpeted with petrified grass, populated with petrified animals and containing even birds petrified in flight. In the hot water springs, they saw fish swimming from the cold water to be boiled alive in the hot water coming from the ground. But there are marvels further west so fabulous that they could not be exaggerated.

Right
Lewis and Clark on the Columbia River in 1805, from the painting by Harold von Schmidt. This expedition explored the unknown wilderness of the Louisiana Purchase.

Inset
The Grand Tetons, a magnificent mountain range that dominates Grand Teton National Park in Wyoming.

Previous page
"The Shrine of Democracy". Sixty foot high portraits of Washington, Jefferson, Lincoln, and Theodore Roosevelt carved into the granite of Mount Rushmore, South Dakota.

Below
The sudden eruption of a geyser alarms nineteenth-century visitors to Yellowstone National Park. Most celebrated of the park's geysers is Old Faithful, so called for its frequent and regular eruptions.

Right
The Upper and Lower Falls of the Yellowstone are two spectacular cataracts which plummet over 400 feet.

Opposite
Bull elk in Yellowstone National Park, Wyoming. Once widely distributed across North America, it was hunted to near extinction by white hunters. The Indians called it wapiti.

When a small party of government surveyors reached a high point overlooking Bryce Canyon in Utah, the view took their breath away. They had seen many natural wonders, but here was something special. T. C. Bailey, the leader of the party, was carried away by the grandeur. "There are thousands of red, white, purple, and vermilion colored rocks of all sizes," he wrote, "resembling sentinels on the walls of castles, monks and priests in their robes, attendants, cathedrals, and congregations. There are deep caverns and rooms resembling ruins of prisons, castles, churches, niches, and recesses, presenting the wildest and most wonderful scene that the eye of man ever beheld." Bailey wrote those words just over a hundred years ago. Driving up to the 9,000 foot high rim in a four-wheel-drive vehicle, astounded visitors still agree with his description.

Utah is a country resplendent with sights of awesome beauty. In the north of the state, the Wasatch and Uinta ranges of the Rocky Mountains dominate the landscape. In the west, there is the vast, lonely region reaching towards the Sierra Nevada Mountains, the last great barrier that faced pioneers on their journey to California. On the border with Arizona is Monument Valley. Covering 1,500 square miles, the valley is studded with sandstone pinnacles, columns and turrets, all shaped by the wind and some rising 2,000 feet above the desert floor. Many film makers, such as John Ford, have featured this dramatic landscape in Westerns, making it the sight most evocative of the Old West. Today, Monument Valley is owned and inhabited by the Navajo Indians. Further along the border is Rainbow Bridge National Monument. Spanning 291 feet, it is the world's largest natural arch.

The Grand Canyon, Arizona, is often called one of the seven wonders of the world. Winding along for some 280 miles, the Colorado river has cut a ravine over a mile deep and up to 14 miles wide. The erosion of the brilliantly multi-colored rock layers is estimated to have taken some ten million years. Within the canyon, there is a range of micro-climates, from cool Canadian weather on the rim to the blistering heat of Mexico at the bottom. The first European to see the canyon was the Spanish conquistador Pedro de Tover. In 1540, a group of Hopi Indians took him to the rim. A better overall view is today obtained from the window of a light aircraft, although a mule ride into the depths of the canyon is guaranteed to give a stronger sense of nature's power.

For hundreds of years after Pedro's discovery, the Grand Canyon remained unexplored. "It seems intended by nature," concluded one pioneer, "that the Colorado river, along the greater part of its lonely and majestic way, shall be forever unvisited and undisturbed." In 1869, however, John Wesley Powell led a small team of four boats on to the dangerous river. Many times were their craft drenched and smashed by the wild rapids. With each loss of food and supplies brought by the bucking white water, the party cheered themselves with the thought, "Well, the boats will be lighter anyway as we go on." With only a few days' rations left, the Powell

expedition burst out into the Grand Wash at the end of their journey. "The river rolls by us in silent majesty; the quiet of the camp is sweet, our joy is almost ecstasy." Now you can experience the thrill of the white water without the danger. Excursions along the Colorado use unsinkable rubber motorboats that bounce over the rapids.

The Powell expedition reveals the danger and fear felt by many of the early explorers on first seeing the natural wonders of the West. Death Valley in California is one of the driest and hottest places in the world. Third largest of the national monuments, 140 miles long and varying from 6 to 20 miles wide, the valley desert was a death trap for early travelers to the west coast. The Indians called the sun-blasted area *Tomesha*, meaning Ground on Fire. In 1849, when the emaciated survivors of a gold rush party made their way out of this anvil of the sun, one of them turned round and said, "Good-bye, Death Valley." The name stuck. And yet, despite the harsh terrain, some people actually chose to make the valley their home. One of them was the eccentric Walter Scott.

Discovering a gold mine in the Death Valley

wilderness, Scott fulfilled a long cherished fantasy. In 1924, he hired a construction team and began to build a castle. With turrets, battlements and a heavy portcullis, it was in every way a medieval European fortress. Inside, craftsmen from Germany and Spain created a baronial hall of rich timber and walls hung with tapestries and fine paintings. Scotty lived in the castle until the age of 82 in 1954, entertaining film stars and politicians and telling them of his days in Buffalo Bill's Wild West Show. Scotty's Castle is one of the top tourist attractions of the Death Valley National Monument.

A less renowned wonder of Death Valley is the Race Track. A dry lake bed high up in the Cottonwood Mountains on the west side of the valley, it is one of its most perplexing natural phenomena. Mysterious tracks are found streaking across the lake bed, ending at rocks of various sizes. Evidence indicates that the rocks, some weighing as much as 600 pounds, skid across the lake bed making trails up to 800 feet long. Geologists have a theory that this movement is caused by high winds, but nobody has completely solved this unique mystery of Death Valley.

Below
Bryce Canyon, Utah. Its natural beauty overwhelmed early explorers who called it "the wildest and most wonderful scene that the eye of man ever beheld".

Opposite above
The Lower Falls in Yellowstone National Park, Wyoming.

Opposite below
The "half-dome" of monolithic granite in the Yosemite National Park, California.

Rocks of an equally amazing character can be seen in the Painted Desert of northern Arizona. Thousands of great logs, brilliant with jasper and agate, lie scattered around the arid terrain. It is the world's biggest and brightest collection of petrified wood. The local Navajo Indians explain this phenomenon with a legend telling of a god who went hunting in the ancient forest that once covered the land. When he wanted to make a fire to cook the game he had slain, he found the wood too damp to burn. So in his anger he cursed the forest and turned it into stone. Geologists, however, tell a different story. Millions of years ago, these trees were buried in mud, sand and volcanic ash. Silica-bearing water then penetrated the wood cells. The water evaporated and the silica turned into quartz.

A petrified log is a treasure chest of gemstones: agate, jasper, opal and amethyst. When polished, a section of petrified wood glows and flashes with many brilliant colors. But not all the natural wonders of the West are monumentally dead. There are many living marvels. In Sequoia National Park in California stand the world's tallest trees. Beginning its growth at the time of the Trojan War, the tallest tree in the Giant Forest is 101 feet around the base and soars to just over 272 feet. It has been estimated that just this one tree could produce 600,000 board feet of timber.

The national parks of the West teem with wildlife. An annual buffalo round-up at the National Bison Range in Montana recalls the old cowboy days. But frequently, fascinating animals can be seen in more humble circumstances. The roadrunner is found throughout the cactus country of the Southwest. In the era of the stagecoach and wagon trains, this comic bird used to race ahead of the vehicles at 18 miles an hour. Today, it has been known to run after balls on a golf course with the eagerness of a dog. From the smallest bird to the deepest canyon, the natural wonders of the West survive to remind us of nature's supremacy in this vast and beautiful land.

Previous page
Triple Arch, Arches National Park, Utah. Centuries upon centuries of wind-blown sand have slowly eroded away the soft stone to leave a hard rock structure

Right
Sequoias in Yosemite National Park, California: the tallest trees in the world, soaring on average to well over 200 feet.

Opposite
Petrified wood in the Petrified Forest National Park, Arizona. Agate and opal have replaced the decayed wood to produce some of the most beautiful of nature's work.

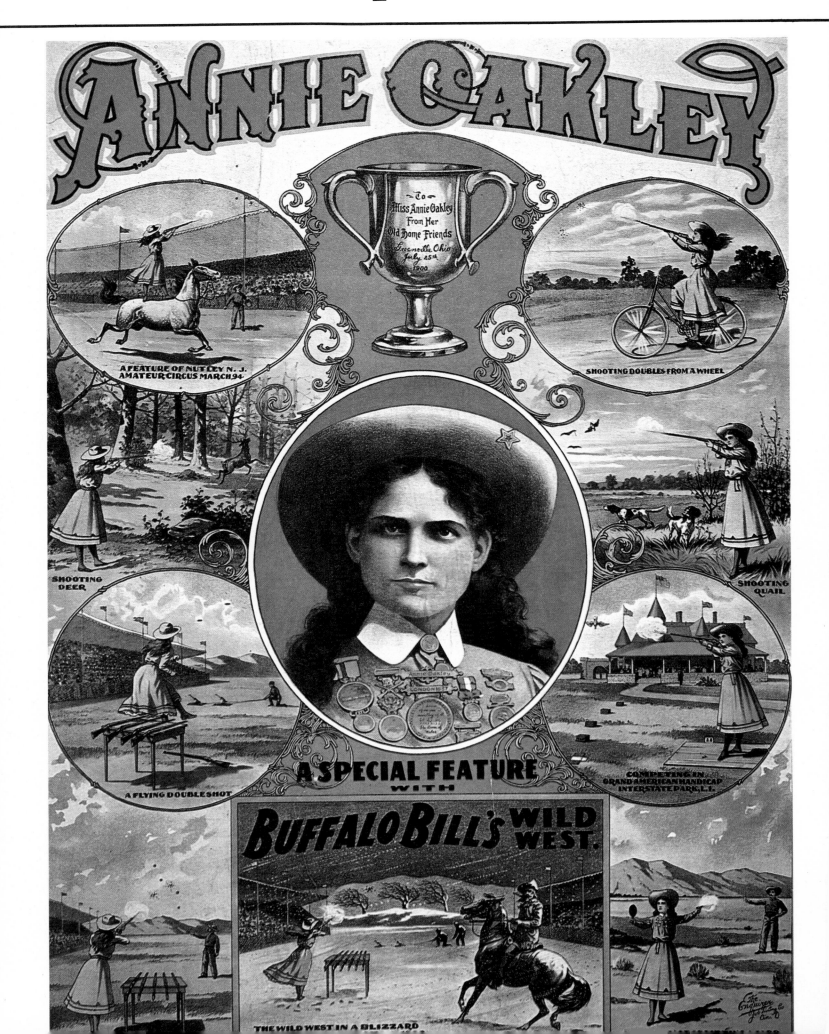

"The cult of the Western is far from finished," says a Hollywood film producer. "Take Luke Skywalker, that's a cowboy name. He carries his laser gun in a holster, just like any frontier hero." Although it might seem that, after a hundred years, the cowboy as a popular hero is giving way to the space warrior, the essential format and style of the Western remains strong. The new frontier is outer space but the earthmen and aliens that contest it are little different from the cowboys and Indians of yesteryear. The pioneer spirit is with us always. In the film *The Right Stuff*, test pilot Chuck Yeager rides out to his fire-roaring X-1 rocket on a horse in a cacti-strewn desert. Surviving on the edge of the wilderness, the cowboy and spaceman have much in common.

But it is not just the characters of the Old West that live on in popular culture; Americans have a yearning for the free, open life of the range. The sophisticated oil heroes and villains of television's *Dallas* live on a ranch in cattle country. They might wear suits beneath their stetsons, but they look forward to a rodeo as much as a candle-lit dinner. The bars and honky-tonks of Houston are packed with office-working urban cowboys testing their staying power on mechanical bucking broncs.

For the more adventurous, the wild lands of the national parks offer a weekend on the frontier. At times, the pioneer fantasy can be shattered by the harsh reality of a wilderness that's bigger and tougher than ever expected. In the film *Deliverance*, Burt Reynolds and his city-slicker friends take a canoe down a river into the far beyond. The white water nearly drowns them and their trip turns into a nightmare of bare survival. The film was not made in the West, but it illustrates the desire of modern Americans to experience the rigors of the wild.

Of course, the Wild West was not a place of romance and excitement for those who actually lived in it a hundred years ago. The cowboy, in particular, was seen more as a villain than a hero. "Whenever a Western town is sacked, or a railroad is robbed by masked men," wrote William M. Thayer in 1888, "it is heralded throughout the eastern States as the crime of the cowboys. Although it is more likely the action of a gang of professionals from New York or Chicago. That there are bad cowboys must be admitted. But as a class, they are not the desperadoes and cut-throats which many eastern papers represent them to be." For most easterners in the nineteenth century, the territory west of the Mississippi was a land of savages, bandits and wild animals. You made a fast buck there if you had to, but as soon as the new transcontinental railroads could get you the hell out of there, you made for the civilization of the East.

A key factor in the romanticizing of the Old

Opposite
A Buffalo Bill's Wild West Show poster featuring sharpshooter Annie Oakley. The Buffalo Bill show toured the US and Europe performing before packed houses, bringing the flavor and color of the Wild West to city folk.

Below
A sallow image of John Wayne in the Wax Museum at Anaheim outside Los Angeles. Wayne was one of the biggest box-office attractions the cinema has known. As he grew older, his rugged features embodied the pioneer spirit.

West was Buffalo Bill's Wild West Show. Featuring real cowboys and Indians, this theatrical spectacle toured North America and Europe for 25 years from its inception in 1883. A typical show included rough-riding and roping by cowboys; a re-enactment of the Deadwood Stagecoach attack by Indians and its rescue in the nick of time by Buffalo Bill on a white horse; sharpshooting by Annie Oakley and the guest appearance of such Western legends as the Indian Chiefs Sitting Bull and Red Cloud. William "Buffalo Bill" Cody began his career in the real West of Kansas. A Pony Express rider at the age of 14, he was hired by the railroad to provide buffalo meat for its workers. In 19 months, he killed more than 4,000 buffalo, hence his nickname. It was his meeting with a writer called Ned Buntline that changed his life and altered the image of the Old West.

Buntline was a writer of dime novels and he turned Buffalo Bill into a popular hero. The fictional exploits of "The greatest scout of the West" were an immediate success. Even the US government was sufficiently impressed by the daring adventures of Buffalo Bill, the first comic-book superman, to award him the Medal of Honor for bravery during a campaign against the Indians. All was not without foundation, however, for in 1876 it was reported that Cody had killed and scalped the Cheyenne Chief Yellow Hand while scouting with the US Fifth Cavalry. Happening as it did just after the US Seventh Cavalry's defeat at Little Bighorn, it was celebrated as "the first scalp for Custer". Acting on stage in a play based on the incident, Cody acquired a taste for the limelight and from there developed his Wild West Show. In 1887, Buffalo Bill performed before Queen Victoria and the Royal Family in London. The Wild West had become the latest rage in popular entertainment. It was destined to become big business.

Films and books spread the romantic image of the Old West throughout the world, so that everyone became familiar with the names of Jesse James, Wild Bill Hickock and Geronimo, even if their exploits weren't exactly clear. The cinema first got on to the Wild West bandwagon in 1903 with *The Great Train Robbery*. Made just two years after Butch Cassidy's Wild Bunch had robbed and dynamited an express car, it caused a sensation. But the Western only really got into its stride a decade later when William S. Hart tried to capture some of the sharp realism of the Old West in his movies. With the character of the cowboy established as a crowd puller, Tom Mix went on to become the most popular of the silent era heroes.

In his immaculate white costume and hat, Tom Mix took the Western cowpoke on fantastic adventures as far-flung as Arabia

Opposite
Buffalo Bill and Chief Sitting Bull. In 1883, the West came East when Buffalo Bill took real cowboys and Indians on the road in his Wild West Show.

Below
Actors recreate a bank raid for the benefit of tourists in Old Tucson, Arizona. A popular entertainment for sightseers.

Left
Urban cowboys test their staying power on a mechanical bull in a Texan club. The spirit of the rodeo can now be enjoyed by weekend cowboys.

Below
Country singer in a Virginia City nightclub, Nevada. Country music is now the most popular aspect of Western culture.

Above left
Clint Eastwood personifies the quiet-spoken, peaceful Westerner who explodes into action and vengeance when provoked by lawless and unjust elements. A modern hero with a hard edge.

Above right
Roy Rogers and Trigger, smartest horse in the movies. Roy Rogers and Gene Autry were the most popular of the singing cowboys who warbled their way through a series of Western adventures.

Opposite
A bandit crushed by cowboy boots. Dramatic Wild West imagery used to great effect in this eye-catching advertisement for the Nocona Boot Company of Nocona, Texas.

and India, making the cowboy an international superman. But there were many real Westerners in these early films. Cowhands traveled from the declining ranches of the Midwest to work as extras and stunt men in Hollywood for five dollars a day. "The movies paid us a lot more for falling off horses," remembered one old stunt man, "than we had ever been paid for staying on them." Some of the stunts were highly dangerous. A favorite with directors was the Dead Man Fall. In this, a length of piano wire, tied to the horse's legs, was anchored to a buried post. Without warning, the rider galloped off until his horse slammed to the ground and he was catapulted out of his saddle.

Sound added punch – often literally – to Westerns, and confirmed the screen appeal of heroes who were short on talk but big on action. It also gave voice to the singing cowboys. Gene Autry and Roy Rogers wowed audiences with a guitar and a song after shooting up the baddies and saving the girl. A popular taste for Western songs closer to Tin Pan Alley than the ballads of the plains proved the launching pad for the great Country and Western music industry. That money could be made from associating a favorite Western hero with any piece of merchandise was soon appreciated by top advertisers.

On radio, Roy Rogers plugged Quaker Oats and Buck Jones sold Grape Nut Flakes. It was believed that cowboys knew best when it came to healthy eating, although in reality they had been more often the very picture of malnutrition. On the side of one cereal packet, the following legend appeared:

"Cowboys learned a long time ago, that to be up at the crack of dawn working hard till noon, it took a good-sized balanced breakfast. We couldn't agree more."

The most potent use of the cowboy in advertising came with the Marlboro Man. He met the advertisers' need for a strong masculine image to sell cigarettes to men. So powerful was the image, that it enabled the company to abandon the symbolic tattoo that had adorned its previous macho models. The Marlboro Man never said a word himself, but by smoking his cigarettes you were invited to join him in Marlboro Country. A rugged, independent life style on the open range. For many people, it was not so much a cigarette that was being sold but an image of escape from an uptight urban scene.

Television kept the Western in front of millions of viewers. John Wayne turned down the lead role in *Gunsmoke* but it made a star out of James Arness. *Bonanza* and *The Virginian* got top ratings and ensured that the cowboy remained a pop figure. This was fine, but a generation brought up on John Wayne was fast giving way to a new one and a fresh approach was needed to fire their imagination. It arrived in the presence of The Man With No Name as Clint Eastwood revived the aura of the silent, mysterious Westerner pitched against Mexicans and Indians. The cowboy was again a cult idol. In 1980, *Time* magazine featured on its cover a Man of the Year in checkered shirt, blue jeans and a tooled leather belt complete with large silver buckle. The man was Ronald Reagan, but his enthusiasm for the Old West had already hit the streets.

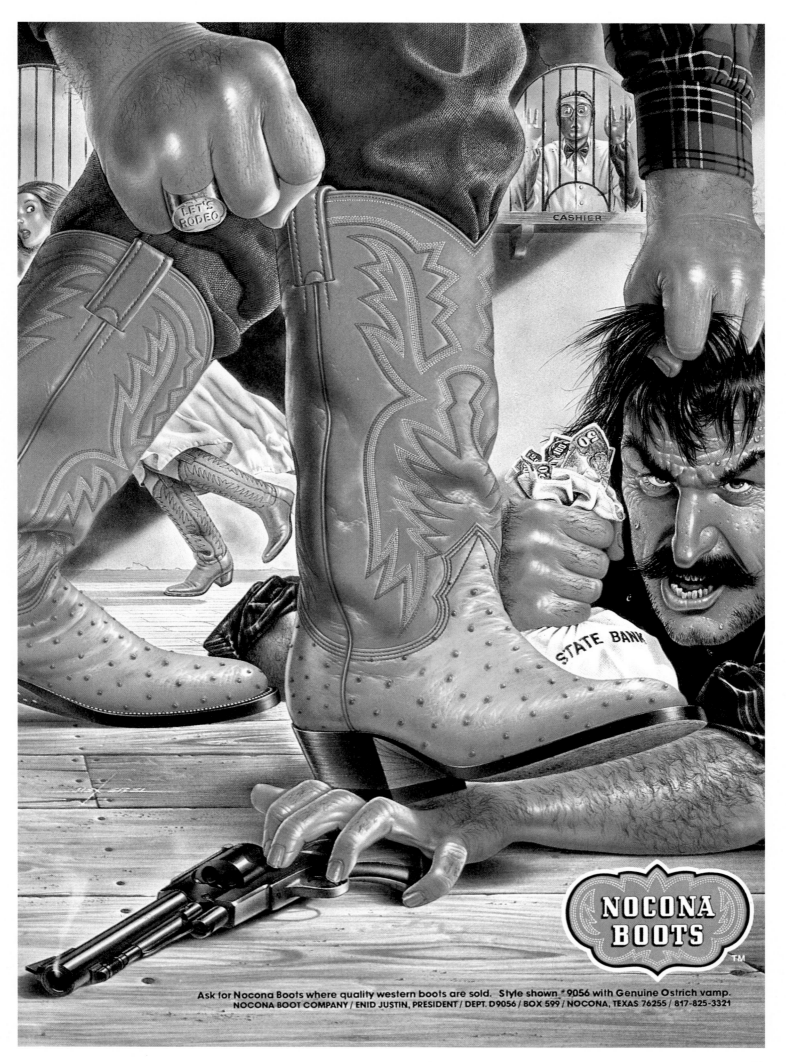

The success of performers such as Charlie Daniels, Willie Nelson and Loretta Lyn made Country and Western the in thing. The Outlaw movement transformed the music of old-timers to the swinging sounds of the dance floor. Across the country, design houses provide the fashions for young urban cowboys and discos have been turned into Western dance halls. In New York, the only full-time FM jazz station was forced to drop that music and become WKHK. It launched a million dollar advertising campaign with posters showing the Statue of Liberty wearing cowboy boots. "The Big Apple hasn't had so much fun in years," it read. "This town is going all out for cowboy boots, chicken fried steak, mechanical bulls and country music on the radio."

Such popularity has altered the character of the authentic honky-tonk. "We don't want no redneck troublemakers here," says an owner of a smart Western club. "We go after the Platinum Cowboys, the ones who drive a Mercedes or a Porsche, wear their cowboy hats on weekends and drink Dewars." But there are still many clubs for the dedicated Westerner. The Lone Star Cafe in New York is one of the most successful. Its Country concerts are syndicated to more than 600 radio stations across the nation.

A hundred years ago, the cultured East Coast hoped to transform the Wild West, but now it seems that American desire to relive the freedom of the frontier days is as vital as ever. Western films, music and fashion are an ever-present link with the life of the wide, open prairie. As one cowboy recently remarked in a Boston nightclub: "Looks like we're gonna Texanize you, before you Americanize us."

Previous page
Cowboys crowd the bar after a rodeo.

Left
The Pioneer Club in Las Vegas. The neon cowboy demonstrates the enduring influence of the Old West theme on the urban scene.

Right
Willie Nelson and Dyan Cannon in the film *Honeysuckle Rose*. Willie Nelson was a leading member of the "Outlaw" music movement that made Country fashionable and attractive to young people.

Upholding the law at a farming fair in Lincoln, Nebraska.

PICTURE CREDITS